PICKLES & CHUTNEYS

First published in Great Britain in 2012 by Bounty Books,
a division of Octopus Publishing Group Ltd
Endeavour House,
189 Shaftesbury Avenue,
London WC2H 8JY
www.octopusbooks.co.uk

An Hachette UK Company
www.hachette.co.uk

Material previously appeared in:
All Colour Cookbook 200 Jams & Preserves published by Hamlyn in 2012
Preserves published by Hamlyn in 2005
Pickles & Preserves published by Bounty Books in 2010

ISBN: 978-0-753723-93-7

A CIP catalogue record for this book is available from the British Library

Printed and bound in China

Measurements: Both metric and imperial measurements are given in all recipes. Use one set of measurements, not a mixture of both.

Standard level spoon measurements are used in all recipes
1 tablespoon = one 15 ml spoon
1 teaspoon = one 5 ml spoon

American cup conversions:

1 cup granulated/caster sugar	225g (8oz)
1 cup demerera/muscovado sugar	200g (7oz)

liquids:

¼ cup	60ml (2 fl oz)
½ cup	120ml (4 fl oz)
1 cup	240ml (8 fl oz)

The recipes in this book use an imperial pint (570ml/20 fl oz). The American pint is 16 fl oz (480ml).

Yield: The yields given for the recipes in this book are approximate.

The recipes in this book have been developed and tested in a home kitchen. Although every effort has been made to convey these recipes as risk-free as possible, the publisher assumes no responsibility for damages associated with the use of this book.

In the US, there are certain guidelines for preserving and canning set out by the food standards agency, USDA. Refer to http://nchfp.uga.edu/publications/publications_usda.html.

Photographs © Octopus Publishing Group, apart from: 9 WaltonCreative/Alamy 25, 37, 49 iStockphoto/Thinkstock 27, 45 Monkey Business/Thinkstock 33 Dream79/Shutterstock 41 dontree/Fotolia 53 By Ian Miles-Flashpoint Pictures/Alamy 57 sarsmis/Fotolia 59 Subbotina Anna/Fotolia

CONTENTS

INTRODUCTION

Making chutneys and pickles is simple and rewarding and these delicious savoury preserves are perfect to serve with a range of dishes.

CHUTNEYS

Chutneys are a cross between a pickle and a jam with a sweet and sour taste.

When making chutneys, simply finely shred or dice fruit or vegetables, or a mix of the two, then put them into a large pan with sugar, vinegar and flavourings and simmer gently until thick. Flavourings can be as simple or exotic as you like.

Choose from Thai-inspired flavours such as ginger and lemongrass, Indian spice blends with turmeric, paprika, cardamom and cumin or Mediterranean mixes of garlic, herbs and juniper.

There is also a second type of chutney that is of Indian origin. These chutneys are uncooked and highly spiced. Fresh-tasting and aromatic, they are an excellent accompaniment to curries, cold meats and barbecued foods and can be kept in the refrigerator for 2 or 3 days. You'll find a recipe for one of these uncooked chutneys, Mango, Apple & Mint, on page 40.

PICKLES

Pickles tend to be made with larger pieces or whole fruit and vegetables steeped in a flavoured and sweetened vinegar. Unlike chutneys, the fruit and vegetables are generally preserved while still raw.

KEY EQUIPMENT

Preserving pan or large saucepan

This should be at least 25 cm (10 inches) in diameter and 11 cm (4½ inches) deep. It needs to be this wide to allow for good evaporation and to give the contents room to cook without boiling over. Preserving pans are available in aluminium, stainless steel, enamel and copper. Copper pans heat up quickly but are unsuitable for making chutney as the vinegar in chutney reacts with the metal. Whichever you choose, make sure it has a thick base as this reduces the chances of your chutney burning.

Spoons

Use a long-handled wooden spoon for stirring, to keep your hand away from the hot preserve. A large ladle is useful when it comes to filling jars with your chutney or pickle.

Jam funnel

Made of metal to withstand the heat of just-cooked preserves, a jam funnel reduces spills down the sides of jars and helps to eliminate scalds when potting preserves. They generally measure 12–15 cm (5–6 inches) across the top.

Jars, bottles and tops

Recycle jam jars for chutneys and pickles. Check all jars carefully before use and throw away any with cracks or chips. Vinegar corrodes metal so choose plastic-coated, screw-top lids. You can also use specialist glass preserving jars with screw-on or clip-on lids also made of glass.

EQUIPMENT CHECKLIST

- Sharp knife and chopping board
- Preserving pan or large saucepan
- Long-handled wooden spoon
- Ladle
- Jam funnel
- Sterilized jars and lids
- Labels

KEY INGREDIENTS

Vinegar

Vinegar is one of the most important ingredients when it comes to making chutneys and pickles. Use a good quality vinegar with an acetic content of at least 5%. Poor quality vinegars contain less acetic acid and so are not good for preserving. The recipes in this book use range of vinegars, including malt, distilled malt, white and red wine, cider, sherry and rice vinegars. You can also buy spiced vinegar to use when making pickles or you could make your own (see box right for recipe).

Sugar

Granulated white sugar, caster sugar, light and dark brown, muscovado and demerara sugar can all be used when making pickles and chutneys. As a rule of thumb, the darker the sugar used, the darker the chutney will be.

THE IMPORTANCE OF STERILIZING

Hygiene is really important when preserving and especially when potting the finished preserves. Make sure jars are well washed, rinsed with hot water and dried, then sterilized in a warm oven for 10 minutes. Alternatively jars can be sterilized on a standard wash cycle in a dishwasher and filled while still warm. Ensure they are dry before filling them.

SPICED VINEGAR

Use this spicy vinegar when making pickles or for salad dressings and sauces with a hidden kick.

makes: 2.25 litres (4 pints)

2.25 litres (4 pints) malt vinegar
1 cinnamon stick
12 cloves
2 tablespoons coriander seeds
1 tablespoon mustard seeds
4 dried red chillies
2 teaspoons black peppercorns

Mix the vinegar in a saucepan with all the spices and heat gently to boiling point. Reduce the heat, cover the pan and simmer the mixture gently for 15 minutes. Leave it to cool. Strain the cooled vinegar through a fine sieve, pour into a sterilized bottle and use it as required.

You should also ensure that you sterilize jam funnels, ladles and screw-top lids.

HOW TO TELL WHEN CHUTNEY IS READY

Here's a simple way to know when your chutney is ready: when you think it is thick enough, draw a wooden spoon across the surface of the chutney. If it leaves a channel behind that does not immediately fill with liquid, then it is done.

BOTTLING YOUR CHUTNEYS AND PICKLES

Ladle the just-cooked chutney or prepared pickle into jars that are still warm but are dry. Fill the jars to the top and press down well. Immediately top with a sterilized, plastic-coated, airtight lid. The lid needs to be airtight not just to keep the bacteria out but to stop the vinegar evaporating. Allow the jars to cool, if necessary, and label each jar to identify its contents and add the date when it was made.

MATURING TIME

Most chutneys and pickles will improve and mellow in flavour as they are stored. Without this maturation time, they are sharp and vinegary. If a recipe benefits from maturing, the time needed is indicated at the end of each recipe

HOW TO STORE CHUTNEYS AND PICKLES

The key to successful and long storage of preserves is a cool, dark place away from direct sunlight. Light will make the colour of the preserve fade and any damp could make it mouldy. Choose a cupboard away from a heat source or a box in a cool garage works well too. Once they are opened, pickles and chutneys should be stored in the refrigerator.

PUMPKIN & WALNUT CHUTNEY

prep time: 30 minutes cooking time: 1½–2 hours makes: 4 jars

- 1 kg (2 lb) pumpkin, weighed after peeling and deseeding
- 2 onions, finely chopped
- 1 large orange, finely chopped, including skin and pith
- 600 ml (1 pint) white wine vinegar
- 375 g (12 oz) granulated sugar
- 1 cinnamon stick, halved
- 5 cm (2 inch) piece root ginger, peeled and finely chopped
- 1 teaspoon turmeric
- 1 teaspoon dried crushed red chillies
- 1 teaspoon salt
- freshly ground black pepper
- 50 g (2 oz) walnut pieces

1 Dice the pumpkin, then add to a preserving pan with all the remaining ingredients. Cover and cook gently for 1 hour, stirring from time to time, until softened. Remove the lid and cook for ½–1 hour, stirring more frequently towards the end of cooking as the chutney thickens.

2 Ladle into warm, dry jars, filling to the very top and pressing down well. Disperse any air pockets with a skewer or small knife and cover with screw-top lids. Label and leave to mature in a cool, dark place for at least 3 weeks.

This chutney is good with blue cheese and fresh, crusty bread for a quick and satisfying lunch.

ALE, APPLE & MUSTARD CHUTNEY

prep time: 30 minutes cooking time: 1¾–2 hours makes: 4 jars

1 kg (2 lb) cooking apples, quartered, cored, peeled and diced
500 g (1 lb) onions, finely chopped
250 g (8 oz) celery, diced
250 g (8 oz) ready diced stoned dates
550 ml bottle brown ale
150 ml (¼ pint) malt vinegar
300 g (10 oz) demerara sugar
2 tablespoons white mustard seeds, roughly crushed
1 teaspoon turmeric
1 teaspoon salt
1 teaspoon black peppercorns, roughly crushed

1 Add all the ingredients to a preserving pan and cook, uncovered, over a gentle heat for 1¾–2 hours, stirring from time to time, but more frequently towards the end of cooking as the chutney thickens.

2 Ladle into warm, dry jars, filling to the very top and pressing down well. Disperse any air pockets with a skewer or small knife and cover with screw-top lids. Label and leave to mature in a cool, dark place for at least 3 weeks.

This chutney is delicious with strong cheese and crunchy fruit and vegetables, such as apples and celery.

GARLICKY MEDITERRANEAN CHUTNEY

prep time: 20 minutes cooking time: 1½ hours makes: 3 jars

- 1 garlic bulb (about 12 cloves), peeled and finely chopped
- 300 g (10 oz) onions, chopped
- 500 g (1 lb) tomatoes, skinned (optional) and roughly chopped
- 500 g (1 lb) courgettes, diced
- 6 peppers of different colours, halved, deseeded and cut into strips
- 250 ml (8 fl oz) red wine vinegar
- 250 g (8 oz) granulated sugar
- 1 tablespoon tomato purée
- 3 stems rosemary, leaves chopped
- salt and freshly ground black pepper

1 Add all the ingredients to a preserving pan and cook, uncovered, over a gentle heat for 1½ hours, stirring from time to time, but more frequently towards the end of cooking as the chutney thickens.

2 Ladle into warm, dry jars, filling to the very top and pressing down well. Disperse any air pockets with a skewer or small knife and cover with screw-top lids.

3 Label and leave to mature in a cool, dark place for at least 3 weeks.

This vibrant chutney makes the very best of summer vegetables and is just the thing to perk up barbecued sausages and burgers.

HONEY PICKLED CHILLIES

prep time: 15 minutes cooking time: 7–8 minutes makes: 2 jars

500 g (1 lb) whole red finger chillies
450 ml (¾ pint) cider or white wine vinegar
4 tablespoons set honey
4 tablespoons light muscovado sugar
4 bay leaves
4 sprigs thyme
4 garlic cloves, peeled and sliced
2.5 cm (1 inch) piece root ginger, peeled and finely chopped
1 teaspoon coriander seeds
1 teaspoon salt

1 Add the chillies to a saucepan of boiling water and cook for 2–3 minutes until just softened. Tip into a colander, rinse with cold water and drain well.

2 Pour the vinegar into the drained pan and add all the remaining ingredients. Heat gently until the sugar has dissolved, then cook over a medium heat for 5 minutes.

3 Pack the chillies and herbs from the vinegar tightly into 2 jars, then pour over the hot vinegar mixture, making sure that the chillies are completely covered by the vinegar. Cover with screw-top lids, label and leave to mature in a cool, dark place for 3–4 weeks.

Honey adds a hint of mellow sweetness to these pickled chillies. Use them to add a burst of flavour to salads, stir-fries and meat dishes.

SPICED PLUM CHUTNEY

prep time: 25 minutes cooking time: 1 hour makes: 2 jars

½ teaspoon cumin seeds
½ teaspoon fennel seeds
1 teaspoon coriander seeds
½ teaspoon dried chilli flakes
1 kg (2 lb) plums, halved, stoned and diced
1 onion, chopped
2.5 cm (1 inch) piece root ginger, peeled and finely chopped
150 ml (¼ pint) malt vinegar
125 g (4 oz) granulated sugar
2 tablespoons raisins
juice of 1 lemon
salt and freshly ground black pepper

1 Crush the seeds roughly in a pestle and mortar, then toast in a hot preserving pan with the chilli flakes for a few seconds. Add all the remaining ingredients, then cover and simmer gently for 30 minutes, stirring from time to time.

2 Uncover the chutney and cook for 30 minutes, stirring until thick and pulpy. Mash with a potato masher, or blitz in a food processor or liquidizer, until smooth.

3 Ladle into warm, dry jars, filling to the very top and pressing down well. Disperse any air pockets with a skewer or small knife and cover with screw-top lids. Label and leave to mature in a cool, dark place for at least 3 weeks.

This spicy and sweet chutney is a great condiment to serve with pork or poultry and is delicious in a cheese salad sandwich.

AUTUMNAL HARVEST CHUTNEY

prep time: 30 minutes cooking time: 1½ hours makes: 6 jars

1 kg (2 lb) mixed green and red tomatoes, roughly chopped
500 g (1 lb) red plums, stoned and roughly chopped
1 marrow (about 750 g/ 1½ lb), peeled, halved, deseeded and diced
500 g (1 lb) onions, roughly chopped
100 g (3½ oz) sultanas or raisins
300 ml (½ pint) distilled malt vinegar
250 g (8 oz) granulated sugar
1 tablespoon tomato purée
2 teaspoons hot paprika
2 teaspoons English mustard powder
1 teaspoon salt
2 teaspoons black peppercorns, roughly crushed

1 Add all the ingredients to a preserving pan, stir to combine, then cook, uncovered, over a gentle heat for 1½ hours, stirring from time to time, but more frequently towards the end of cooking as the chutney thickens.

2 Ladle into warm, dry jars, filling to the very top and pressing down well. Disperse any air pockets with a skewer or small knife and cover with screw-top lids. Label and leave to mature in a cool, dark place for at least 3 weeks.

This traditional chutney is the ideal way to use up a glut of seasonal vegetables and make them last all year.

PICKLED WALNUTS

prep time: 10 minutes + soaking and standing cooking time: 15 minutes makes: 4–5 jars

500 g (1 lb) young fresh walnuts
50 g (2 oz) salt
600 ml (1 pint) water
3 level teaspoons mixed pickling spice
1.7 litres (3 pints) white wine vinegar

1 Using a silver fork, prick each walnut deeply in 2 or 3 places.

2 To make the brine, add the salt to the water and stir to mix. Add the walnuts, ensuring they are covered in the brine, place a plate on top to keep them submerged and soak them for 14 days.

3 Remove the walnuts from the brine and place on a tray or cloth in the sun, shaking them occasionally. They will turn black after 2 or 3 days, or in 24 hours if it is very hot.

4 Meanwhile, make the spiced vinegar. Put the mixed pickling spice and vinegar into a pan and boil for 15 minutes. Strain and leave until cold.

5 When the walnuts are quite black, pack into warm, dry jars and cover with the spiced vinegar. Top with screw-top lids. Label and leave to mature in a cool, dark place for at least 1 month before using, or store, unopened, for 3–4 months.

Use only young walnuts for this recipe; if they are over-ripe they will not pickle. Serve with both cold meats and most varieties of cheese – the textures of ripe Brie or Camembert are very complementary.

RED TOMATO CHUTNEY

prep time: 30 minutes   cooking time: 1½ hours   makes: 3–4 jars

---

1 kg (2 lb) ripe tomatoes
225 g (8 oz) sultanas
500 g (1 lb) onions
175 g (6 oz) muscovado sugar
1½ teaspoons ground coriander
1½ teaspoons ground ginger
2 cloves garlic, crushed
175 ml (6 fl oz) malt vinegar

1 Place the tomatoes in a large bowl, cover with boiling water and allow them to stand for 30 seconds. Then drain, peel and chop them, together with the sultanas. Finely chop the onions. Mix all the ingredients in a large preserving pan and bring to the boil, stirring continuously.

2 Cover the pan, reduce the heat and simmer for 1¼ hours, stirring occasionally to make sure it does not stick to the pan. Uncover the pan and continue to cook for a further 15 minutes.

3 Transfer the chutney to warm, dry jars and cover with screw-top lids. Label and leave to mature in a cool, dark place for at least 1 month.

PICCALILLI

prep time: 30 minutes + standing cooking time: 25 minutes makes: 2–3 jars

1 small cauliflower
½ cucumber
2 onions
2 large carrots
about 50 g (2 oz) salt
2 tablespoons plain flour
300 ml (½ pint) cider vinegar
225 g (8 oz) granulated sugar
½ teaspoon turmeric
3 teaspoons ground ginger
2 teaspoons English mustard powder
freshly ground black pepper

1 Trim the outer leaves from the cauliflower and break it into small florets, discarding any large stalks. Thinly peel and roughly chop the cucumber. Chop the onions and cut the carrots into medium chunks. Place all the prepared vegetables in layers in a large bowl, sprinkling each layer with salt, and leave them to stand overnight. Lightly rinse and thoroughly dry them.

2 Mix the flour to a smooth cream with a little of the vinegar. Heat the remaining vinegar in a preserving pan with the sugar, spices and mustard, stirring until the sugar has dissolved. Bring to the boil, season the mixture generously with pepper and add the vegetables. Return it to the boil, then reduce the heat and simmer, uncovered, for 10 minutes.

3 Remove the pan from the heat and gradually stir in the flour mixture. Return it to the heat, bring the pickle to the boil and cook it gently for a further 5 minutes. Transfer the piccalilli to warm, dry jars, cover with screw-top lids and label. Piccalilli is ready to eat as soon as it is made.

This pickle is traditionally very spicy with a crunchy texture. Celery and green beans may also be added to the ingredients.

SWEET PICKLED CUCUMBERS

prep time: 25 minutes + soaking cooking time: 5–6 minutes makes: 3 jars

2 large cucumbers, thinly sliced
1 medium onion, thinly sliced
50 g (2 oz) salt
450 ml (¾ pint) white wine vinegar
375 g (12 oz) granulated sugar
½ teaspoon turmeric
2 teaspoons fennel seeds
½ teaspoon dried crushed red chillies
¼ teaspoon black peppercorns, roughly crushed

1 Layer the cucumbers, onions and salt in a bowl, cover with a plate and weight down, then leave to soak for 4 hours.

2 Meanwhile, pour the vinegar into a preserving pan, add the sugar and the remaining ingredients and heat gently, stirring from time to time, until the sugar has dissolved, then leave to cool.

3 Tip the cucumber and onions into a colander and drain off the liquid. Rinse with plenty of cold water and drain well.

4 Reheat the vinegar mixture until just boiling, add the drained cucumber and onion, cook for 1 minute, then lift out of the vinegar with a draining spoon and pack into warm, dry jars. Boil the remaining vinegar mixture for 4–5 minutes until syrupy, then leave to cool.

5 Pour the cold vinegar mixture over the cucumber slices to completely cover and to fill the jars to the top (adding a little extra vinegar if needed). Screw on lids, label and leave to mature in a cool, dark place for 3–4 weeks.

PICKLED SHALLOTS

prep time: 30 minutes + soaking and standing cooking time: 5 minutes makes: 1 very large jar

625 g (1¼ lb) small shallots
40 g (1½ oz) salt
450 ml (¾ pint) sherry vinegar
125 g (4 oz) caster sugar
125 g (4 oz) light muscovado sugar
2 garlic cloves, unpeeled
4 small bay leaves
4 sprigs thyme
4 sprigs rosemary
pinch of salt
½ teaspoon black peppercorns, roughly crushed

1 Trim a little off the tops and roots of the shallots, then put into a bowl and cover with boiling water. Leave to soak for 3 minutes, then pour off the water and re-cover with cold water. Lift the shallots out one at a time and peel off the brown skins. Drain and layer in a bowl with the salt. Leave overnight.

2 Tip the shallots into a colander and drain off as much liquid as possible. Rinse with cold water, drain and dry with kitchen towel.

3 Add the vinegar and sugar to a saucepan with the garlic cloves, half the herbs, a pinch of salt and peppercorns. Heat gently until the sugar dissolves, stirring from time to time. Increase the heat to medium and simmer for 5 minutes. Leave to cool.

4 Pack the shallots tightly into warm, dry jars with the remaining herbs. Strain and pour the cold vinegar syrup over the shallots, making sure that the shallots are covered with the vinegar to the very top. Cover with screw-top lids. Label and leave to mature in a cool, dark place for 3–4 weeks.

RED ONION & RAISIN CHUTNEY

prep time: 15 minutes cooking time: 35–40 minutes makes: 3 jars

---

3 tablespoons extra virgin olive oil
1.5 kg (3 lb) red onions, halved and thinly sliced
250 g (8 oz) soft light brown sugar
300 ml (½ pint) red wine vinegar
200 g (7 oz) raisins
3 garlic cloves, finely chopped
3 bay leaves
1 tablespoon wholegrain mustard
½ teaspoon pimenton (smoked hot paprika)
½ teaspoon salt
freshly ground black pepper

1 Heat the oil in a preserving pan, add the onions and cook gently for 10 minutes until softened but not browned.

2 Stir in 3 tablespoons of the sugar and fry gently for 15 minutes, stirring until just beginning to brown.

3 Add the rest of the sugar and the other remaining ingredients, mix well and simmer, uncovered, for 10–15 minutes, stirring occasionally, until the onions are soft and the liquid has reduced and thickened.

4 Transfer the chutney to warm, dry jars and cover with screw-top lids. Label and leave to mature in a cool, dark place for at least 3 weeks.

This tasty preserve is quick and easy to prepare and cook. Serve on toast topped with grilled Cheddar or goats' cheese or spice up a simple ham or cold turkey sandwich.

TORSHI

prep time: 30 minutes + soaking and standing cooking time: 2 minutes makes: 3 assorted jars

- 200 g (7 oz) courgettes, sliced
- 200 g (7 oz) carrots, sliced
- 150 g (5 oz) French beans, halved
- 1 fennel bulb, sliced
- 1 cauliflower, cut into small florets
- 250 g (8 oz) small pickling onions, peeled
- 100 g (3½ oz) salt
- 1 litre (1¾ pints) distilled malt vinegar or white wine vinegar
- 250 g (8 oz) granulated sugar
- 2 teaspoons caraway seeds
- 2 teaspoons coriander seeds, roughly crushed
- ½ teaspoon black peppercorns, roughly crushed
- 6 small dried red chillies
- 6 garlic cloves, peeled and halved
- 4 stems dill or fennel

1 Layer the vegetables in a bowl with the salt, cover with a plate and weight down, then leave to soak overnight.

2 Pour the vinegar into a saucepan and add the sugar, caraway seeds, coriander seeds and peppercorns, then the dried chillies, garlic and 3 stems of dill or fennel. Bring to the boil, stirring until the sugar has dissolved, then set aside for the flavours to mingle.

3 Next day, drain off the liquid from the vegetables, rinse with cold water, drain well, then pat dry with kitchen paper. Pack into warm, dry jars with the halved garlic and chillies from the vinegar mixture and the remaining fresh dill or fennel. Discard the cooked herbs from the spiced vinegar, then pour the cold vinegar mixture into the jars to the very top of the jars, making sure that the vegetables are completely covered (there is no need to strain the vinegar first).

4 Secure the lids, label and leave to mature in a cool, dark place for 3–4 weeks.

PICKLED GARLIC

prep time: 30 minutes   cooking time: 10 minutes + cooling   makes: 6 garlic heads

---

1.2 litres (2 pints) water
300 ml (½ pint) distilled white wine vinegar
50 g (2 oz) granulated sugar
1 tablespoon salt
6 heads of garlic, separated into cloves and peeled

1 Bring the water, vinegar, sugar and salt to the boil in a saucepan, then reduce the heat and simmer for 5 minutes.

2 Add the garlic to the pan, return to the boil and boil hard for 1 minute.

3 Remove the pan from the heat, allow the garlic mixture to cool, then transfer to containers and top with airtight lids. Label and leave to mature in the refrigerator for 10 days before using, or store, unopened, for 6 months.

Many people assume that garlic always has a very strong, intense flavour, but this mellows over time. Pickled garlic can be added to meat and vegetable dishes or stocks, or try them by themselves.

PUMPKIN & RED PEPPER CHUTNEY

prep time: 30 minutes cooking time: 1¼ hours makes: 3 jars

1 kg (2 lb) pumpkin, weighed after peeling and deseeding, sliced
2 red peppers, quartered, deseeded and cored
500 g (1 lb) shallots, peeled, halved if large
3 bay leaves
3 tablespoons extra virgin olive oil
400 ml (14 fl oz) cider or white wine vinegar
125 g (4 oz) granulated sugar
125 g (4 oz) light muscovado sugar
1 teaspoon allspice berries, roughly crushed
½ teaspoon salt
½ teaspoon cayenne pepper

1 Add the pumpkin, red peppers and shallots to a large roasting tin. Tuck the bay leaves in among the vegetables, then drizzle with the oil. Roast in a preheated oven, 200°C (400°F), Gas Mark 6, for 45 minutes until the vegetables are tender and browned.

2 Leave to cool slightly, then remove the skins from the peppers. Roughly chop the peppers, pumpkin and shallots, discarding the bay leaves. Add the vegetables and any juices from the roasting to a preserving pan. Add all the remaining ingredients, then bring to the boil and simmer, uncovered, for about 30 minutes, stirring more frequently towards the end of cooking, until thick.

3 Ladle into warm, dry jars, filling to the very top and pressing down well. Disperse any air pockets with a skewer or small knife and cover with screw-top lids. Label and leave to mature in a cool, dark place for at least 3 weeks.

MANGO, APPLE & MINT CHUTNEY

prep time: 10 minutes makes: about 200 g (7 oz)

- 1 raw green mango, peeled, stoned and roughly chopped
- 1 small apple, peeled, cored and roughly chopped
- 1 teaspoon sea salt
- 1 tablespoon chopped mint leaves
- 1 teaspoon mild chilli powder
- 1 teaspoon soft light brown sugar
- 150 ml (¼ pint) water

1 Put all the ingredients into a food processor or blender and process until smooth.

2 Transfer the chutney to a small serving dish, cover and chill until required.

This chutney would make a tasty accompaniment to any meal, but is particularly delicious served with spicy fish cakes, samosas and lentil- or potato-based curries.

JAPANESE PICKLED GINGER

prep time: 15 minutes + standing cooking time: 3–4 minutes makes: 2 small jars

---

500 g (1 lb) root ginger, peeled and very thinly sliced
50 g (2 oz) salt
250 ml (8 fl oz) rice vinegar
100 g (3½ oz) granulated sugar
2 Thai green or red chillies, sliced
10 white peppercorns

1 Layer the ginger and salt in a bowl, cover with a plate, weight down and leave to stand overnight.

2 Tip the ginger into a colander and drain off as much liquid as possible. Rinse with cold water, drain and dry with kitchen towel.

3 Add the vinegar, sugar, chilli slices and peppercorns to a saucepan, heat gently until the sugar has dissolved, then bring to the boil and cook over a medium heat for 2–3 minutes. Add the ginger and cook for 1 minute.

4 Pack the ginger and hot syrup into warm, dry jars, pressing the ginger below the vinegar mixture so that it is completely covered and the jar filled to the very top. Cover with screw-top lids. Label and leave to mature in a cool, dark place for 3–4 weeks.

Pickled ginger, known as gari in Japan, is a traditional accompaniment for sushi and is believed to cleanse the palate.

HOT LIME PICKLE

prep time: 10 minutes + standing cooking time: 1½ hours makes: 1 large jar

---

6 limes
2 tablespoons salt
2 teaspoons chilli powder
1 tablespoon garam masala
2 tablespoons granulated sugar
6 cloves garlic, crushed
3 large onions
150 ml (¼ pint) vegetable oil
300 ml (½ pint) malt vinegar

1 Roughly chop the limes and place them in a large basin. Mix the salt with the chilli powder, garam masala, sugar and garlic. Sprinkle this mixture over the limes and toss them well in it to coat them thoroughly. Cover the basin and leave the limes to marinate for at least 24 hours – better still, leave them for three days.

2 Finely chop the onions. Heat the oil in a saucepan, add the onions and cook them until soft but not browned. Stir in the chopped limes with their juices and scrape all the spices out of the basin into the pan.

3 Cook the mixture in the oil, stirring continuously, for about 15 minutes. Pour in the vinegar and bring the pickle to the boil. Cover the pan and simmer it for 1 hour, stirring frequently to prevent the mixture from sticking to the bottom of the pan.

4 Ladle the pickle into warm, dry jars, pressing the lime well down into liquid. Cover each jar with a screw-top lid. Label and leave to mature in a cool, dark place for 2 weeks.

SWEET POTATO & ORANGE CHUTNEY

prep time: 30 minutes cooking time: 1¾–2 hours makes: 5 jars

750 g (1½ lb) sweet potatoes, peeled and diced
500 g (1 lb) onions, chopped
250 g (8 oz) sultanas
250 g (8 oz) carrots, coarsely grated
2 oranges, finely chopped, including pith and peel
4 garlic cloves, finely chopped
45 g sachet tamarind pulp
300 g (10 oz) light muscovado sugar
750 ml (1¼ pints) distilled malt vinegar
1½ teaspoons dried crushed chillies
1 teaspoon salt
1 teaspoon black peppercorns, roughly crushed

1 Add all the ingredients to a preserving pan, cover and cook gently for 1 hour, stirring from time to time. Remove the lid and cook for ¾–1 hour, stirring more frequently towards the end of cooking as the chutney thickens.

2 Ladle into warm, dry jars, filling to the very top and pressing down well. Disperse any air pockets with a skewer or small knife and cover with screw-top lids. Label and leave to mature in a cool, dark place for at least 3 weeks.

This unusual chutney combines the sweetness of oranges and sweet potatoes with the tang of tamarind pulp and will enhance any cheeseboard.

RED PEPPER PICKLE

prep time: 30 minutes cooking time: about 2 hours makes: 3 jars

3 large red peppers
450 g (1 lb) cooking apples
450 g (1 lb) onions
225 g (8 oz) dates
225 g (8 oz) dark soft brown sugar
300 ml (½ pint) malt vinegar
½ teaspoon salt

1 Halve the peppers, remove the seeds, pith and stalks and chop the flesh. Peel, core and slice the cooking apples and chop the onions and dates. Mix all the ingredients in a large saucepan and bring the pickle slowly to the boil.

2 Reduce the heat, cover the pan and cook the pickle for 1 hour, stirring occasionally, then remove the lid and continue to simmer it for about 45 minutes. By this time, most of the excess moisture should have evaporated to leave a thickened pickle.

3 Ladle the pickle into warm, dry jars. Cover each jar with a screw-top lid. Label and leave to mature in a cool, dark place for at least 2 weeks.

Red and green peppers give a strong, excellent flavour to chutneys and pickles. The combination of dates and peppers in this pickle makes it the perfect accompaniment to mild cheeses, quiches and cold pork.

MANGO & PINEAPPLE CHUTNEY

prep time: 30 minutes cooking time: 20 minutes makes: 3 jars

- **300 ml (½ pint) distilled malt vinegar**
- **375 g (12 oz) granulated sugar**
- **2 garlic cloves, finely chopped**
- **5 cm (2 inch) piece root ginger, peeled and finely chopped**
- **4 dried chillies, finely chopped**
- **½ teaspoon ground allspice**
- **1 teaspoon salt**
- **1 teaspoon mixed peppercorns, roughly crushed**
- **1 large pineapple, trimmed, peeled, cored and finely chopped in a food processor**
- **2 large, firm, unripe mangoes, peeled, stoned and sliced**

1 Add the vinegar, sugar, garlic and ginger to a preserving pan, then add the dried chillies, allspice, salt and peppercorns. Heat gently, stirring from time to time, until the sugar has dissolved, then simmer gently for 10 minutes so that the flavours mingle together.

2 Stir in the pineapple and sliced mango and cook over a medium heat for 10 minutes until the mango is just translucent and the liquid is syrupy.

3 Ladle into warm, dry jars, filling to the very top. Press the mango slices beneath the syrup, then cover with screw-top lids. Label and leave to mature in a cool, dark place for at least 3 weeks.

The perfect partner for Indian snacks such as poppadoms and pakoras, this spicy chutney will add a kick to grilled chicken or fish too.

PLUM & PEAR CHUTNEY

prep time: 30 minutes cooking time: 1½ hours makes: 3–4 jars

- 1 kg (2 lb) pears
- 1 kg (2 lb) plums
- 500 g (1 lb) onions, chopped
- 300 ml (½ pint) Spiced Vinegar (see page 7)
- 2 cloves garlic, crushed
- 2 tablespoons grated fresh root ginger
- 225 g (8 oz) dates
- 225 g (8 oz) dark soft brown sugar

1 Peel, halve and core the pears. Slice and place them in a preserving pan. Halve and stone the plums and add them to the pan followed by the chopped onion and the vinegar. Add the garlic and ginger and stir well. Chop the dates and stir them into the mixture together with the sugar.

2 Bring the chutney to the boil, cover the pan and reduce the heat, then simmer it for 1½ hours. Stir it occasionally during cooking to prevent it from sticking to the bottom of the pan.

3 Ladle into warm, dry jars, filling to the very top and pressing down well. Disperse any air pockets with a skewer or small knife and cover with screw-top lids. Label and leave to mature in a cool, dark place for at least 2 weeks.

Combine the piquant flavour of plums with the delicate pears to make a delicious chutney for serving with most cold roast meats, particularly pork, and the stronger mature Cheddars.

PICKLED PEACHES

prep time: 25 minutes cooking time: 6–8 minutes makes: 1 large jar

300 ml (½ pint) white malt vinegar
500 g (1 lb) granulated sugar
1 teaspoon whole cloves
1 teaspoon whole allspice berries
7 cm (3 inch) piece cinnamon stick, halved
1 kg (2 lb) small peaches, halved and stoned

1 Pour the vinegar into a large saucepan, add the sugar and spices and heat gently until the sugar has dissolved.

2 Add the peach halves and cook very gently for 4–5 minutes until just tender but still firm. Lift out of the syrup with a slotted spoon and pack tightly into a warm, dry large jar.

3 Boil the syrup for 2–3 minutes to concentrate the flavours, then pour over the fruit, making sure that the fruit is completely covered and the jar filled to the very top. Top up with a little extra warm vinegar if needed. Add a small piece of crumpled greaseproof paper to stop the fruit from rising out of the vinegar in the jar. Screw or clip on the lid, label and leave to cool.

4 After a few hours, the peaches will begin to rise in the jar, but as they become saturated with the syrup they will sink once more; at this point they will be ready to eat.

These peaches go well with slices of ham. You can also use nectarines instead of peaches for this recipe.

APRICOT CHUTNEY

prep time: 20 minutes + standing cooking time: 2–2½ hours makes: 3 jars

500 g (1 lb) dried apricots
500 g (1 lb) onions
2 cloves garlic, crushed
1 red chilli, thinly sliced
½ teaspoon turmeric
1 teaspoon English mustard powder
225 g (8 oz) granulated sugar
600 ml (1 pint) cider vinegar

1 Chop the apricots and onions and mix them together in a preserving pan. Add all the remaining ingredients and stir well, then allow the mixture to stand for 2 hours.

2 Heat the chutney gently, stirring continuously until the sugar has dissolved, bring it to the boil and reduce the heat. Cover the pan and simmer the chutney for about 2 hours, stirring occasionally to make sure it does not stick to the pan. The fruit should be thoroughly softened and the chutney thickened.

3 Ladle into warm, dry jars, filling to the very top and pressing down well. Disperse any air pockets with a skewer or small knife and cover with screw-top lids. Label and leave to mature in a cool, dark place for at least 3 weeks.

This is a delicious, fruity chutney, ideal for serving with roast pork, lamb and duck. It also makes a good side dish with hot curries and other highly spiced dishes.

GINGERED PEAR PICKLE

prep time: 30 minutes cooking time: 1–1½ hours makes: 3 jars

1 kg (2 lb) pears
1 green pepper
2 large onions
100 g (4 oz) dates
2 tablespoons finely chopped root ginger
175 g (6 oz) granulated sugar
300 ml (½ pint) malt vinegar
salt and freshly ground black pepper

1 Peel, core and slice the pears into a preserving pan. Remove the stalk, pith and seeds from the pepper and chop the flesh, together with the onions. Add them to the pan. Chop the dates and stir these in, followed by the ginger, sugar and vinegar. Add a generous sprinkling of salt and pepper and bring the pickle slowly to the boil.

2 Reduce the heat and simmer the pickle, uncovered, for about 1 hour or until the slices of pear are very soft and the preserve has thickened. Stir the mixture frequently during cooking to prevent it from sticking to the pan.

3 Ladle the pickle into warm, dry jars. Cover each jar with a screw-top lid. Label and leave to mature in a cool, dark place for at least 2 weeks.

Pears, often plentiful and cheap in the shops, make a deliciously well-flavoured pickle to serve with meat salads, cold roast meats and pies and hot grills and barbecues.

PEACH & DATE CHUTNEY

prep time: 10 minutes cooking time: 50 minutes makes: 3–4 jars

---

12 peaches
500 g (1 lb) onions, finely chopped
2 garlic cloves, crushed
2 tablespoons grated root ginger
125 g (4 oz) pitted dates, chopped
250 g (8 oz) demerara sugar
300 ml (½ pint) red wine vinegar
salt and freshly ground black pepper

1 Place the peaches in a large bowl, cover with boiling water and leave to stand for about 1 minute, then drain and peel. Halve and stone the fruit and cut into thick slices.

2 Add the onions to a preserving pan with the peaches, garlic, ginger, dates, sugar and vinegar. Add a generous sprinkling of salt and pepper and bring to the boil, stirring continuously, until the sugar has completely dissolved.

3 Reduce the heat and simmer, covered, stirring frequently, for 45 minutes, until the chutney has thickened.

4 Ladle into warm, dry jars. Disperse any air pockets with a skewer or small knife and cover with screw-top lids. Label and leave to mature in a cool, dark place for at least 3 weeks.

GREEN BEAN CHUTNEY

prep time: 25 minutes cooking time: about 35 minutes makes: 6 jars

---

1 kg (2 lb) green beans, trimmed
900 ml (1½ pints) distilled malt vinegar
750 g (1½ lb) demerara sugar
500 g (1 lb) onions, chopped
1½ tablespoons turmeric
1½ tablespoons English mustard powder
3 tablespoons black mustard seeds
3 tablespoons cornflour
1 teaspoon salt
freshly ground black pepper
3 tablespoons water

1 Half-fill a preserving pan with water, bring to the boil, then add the green beans. Return to the boil and cook for 3 minutes. Drain into a colander, refresh with cold water, then drain again. Thinly slice the beans or roughly chop in a food processor.

2 Add the vinegar and sugar to the drained preserving pan, then add the onions. Cover and bring to the boil, then reduce the heat and simmer for 10 minutes.

3 Mix the remaining dry ingredients together in a bowl, then stir in the water until smooth. Stir this into the vinegar mixture, then simmer, uncovered, for 10 minutes, stirring until smooth and thickened.

4 Stir the blanched beans into the vinegar mixture and cook gently for 10 minutes, stirring frequently until just tender. Ladle into warm, dry jars, pressing the beans down well in the vinegar mix. Disperse any air pockets with a skewer or small knife and cover with screw-top lids. Label and leave to mature in a cool, dark place for at least 3 weeks.

INDEX